SHOW-ME

MW00989529

The Missouri Department of Conservation's mission is to protect and manage the fish, forest and wildlife resources of the state; to serve the public and facilitate their participation in resource management activities; and to provide opportunity for all citizens to use, enjoy and learn about fish, forest and wildlife resources.

There are many ways to support the Department's mission.
Visit www.MissouriConservation.org to learn how you can help.

ISBN 978-1-887247-70-2

© 2010, 2017 by the Conservation Commission of the State of Missouri

Equal opportunity to participate in and benefit from programs of the Missouri Department of Conservation is available to all individuals without regard to their race, color, national origin, sex, age or disability. Questions should be directed to the Department of Conservation, PO Box 180, Jefferson City, MO 65102, 573-751-4115 (voice) or 800-735-2966 (TTY), or to the U.S. Fish and Wildlife Service Division of Federal Assistance, 4401 N. Fairfax Drive, Mail Stop: MBSP-4020, Arlington, VA 22203.

An uncommonly
colorful guide
to 50 cool
amphibians
and reptiles
in Missouri

SHOW-ME

Herps

Serving nature and you

by John Miller | *illustrations by* Steve Buchanan

edited by Carol Davit | *designed by* Tracy Ritter | *technical review by* Jeff Briggler

Every child should have mud pies, grasshoppers, waterbugs, tadpoles, frogs, mud-turtles . . . brooks to wade in, pinecones, rocks to roll, sand, snakes, huckleberries and hornets; and any child who has been deprived of these has been deprived of the best part of his education.
—Luther Burbank (1849–1926), American botanist, horticulturalist and pioneer of agricultural science

This book is for anyone curious about Missouri's diverse and fascinating amphibians and reptiles.

Show-Me Herps will introduce you to some of the most interesting amphibians and reptiles you might encounter across the Show-Me State. Whether you are an outdoors person or not, this book will help you learn more about Missouri's amphibians and reptiles and why they are an important part of our natural world.

Part One explains what "herps" means! It describes what amphibians and reptiles have in common and what makes them different. This part of the book also tells you how these animals grow, look and act. It also explains how and where to find, study and conserve them.

Part Two features 18 of the 43 species of amphibians native to Missouri—our salamanders, toads and frogs.

Part Three features 32 of the 69 species of reptiles native to Missouri—our turtles, lizards and snakes.

Parts Two and Three both have illustrations and lots of fun facts about these animals.

At the end of this book you will find a glossary of words associated with amphibians and reptiles, an index of the animals featured in this book and a list of references to help you learn more about herps in Missouri and outside the state.

CONTENTS

6

HERPS AND HERPETOLOGY

"Herps" is a short way of saying "amphibians and reptiles." "Herps" comes from the word "herpetology" (from the Greek: *herpeto-* "animals that creep" and *-logos* "to study"). Herpetology means the study of animals that creep (move with the belly to the ground). People who study and work to conserve amphibians and reptiles are called herpetologists or "herpers."

Amphibians and reptiles are often grouped together—not only because they creep—but also because they are vertebrates (all have backbones), have similar heart structure and often share habitats. Both also are "ectothermic," meaning they must rely on the environment to stay cool or warm. In addition, most herps, but not all, lay eggs.

8

There are
EXCEPTIONS
to every rule!

Throughout Part One, whenever you see the #▶ symbol you can learn about an amphibian that spends its *entire* life in water, a reptile that doesn't lay eggs or another herp that looks, grows or acts differently from other amphibians and reptiles.

HOW AMPHIBIANS AND REPTILES DIFFER

Amphibians and reptiles are different in many ways, however. Amphibians are in the class Amphibia and reptiles in the class Reptilia. "Amphibia" means "dual life," referring to the fact that amphibians spend part of their lives in the water (or moist areas) and some of their lives on land. **1▶** "Reptilia" comes from *repere*, Latin for "to creep." Turtles, snakes and lizards are the reptiles native to Missouri.

Amphibians that live in Missouri are salamanders, toads and frogs. For the most part, all Missouri amphibians have moist skin and no scales. They lay eggs—which are covered with a jelly-like substance—in water. Most amphibians undergo a metamorphosis between larva and adult **2▶**.

Reptiles native to Missouri are turtles, snakes and lizards. As a group, reptiles have skin covered by scales and lay eggs—which have a leathery covering—on land **3▶**. Unlike amphibians, reptiles do not undergo a metamorphosis between hatchling and adult.

EXCEPTIONS

1▶ The hellbender and mudpuppy never leave the water. They remain aquatic their entire lives. The western slimy salamander does not go to water to lay its eggs. It lays them in moist rotten logs, leaf litter or other cover.

2▶ The mudpuppy appears to never complete its life cycle. It reproduces with little or no apparent change from its larval stage. This life style is called neotenic. The western slimy salamander does not go to water because it has no larval stage. The young emerge from the eggs looking like small versions of the adults.

3▶ Some snakes, such as watersnakes, the gartersnake and venomous snakes, do not lay eggs; they have live young.

9

HERPS ARE AMAZING!

Every habitat across Missouri is home to one or more species of amphibians and reptiles. Herps come in a variety of shapes, sizes and colors. Some amphibians have lungs; some have gills; and some absorb oxygen through the skin! Some reptiles—glass lizards and snakes—have no legs, yet they can travel as well as many legged animals. Snakes hear few if any sounds through the air, yet they can feel vibrations from the ground. Snakes also have an extremely keen sense of smell that is far better than ours. All herps have fascinating physical adaptations and behaviors to help them evade predators and survive many harsh environments.

Even though most amphibians and reptiles are predators, for the most part they do their best to avoid people—they do not view us as food! None are at the top of the food chain and yet some people hope never to encounter them. Learning about herps helps people understand that these fascinating animals should not be feared, but appreciated and conserved.

JOHN MILLER

HERPS ENRICH OUR LIVES

Many of us share similar habitats with herps, and so we may briefly encounter them around our homes or farms, or while hiking, fishing or camping. If you are willing to look around your area, whether you live in the city or the country, you probably won't have to go too far to enjoy our native herps. Some people welcome the chance to see a toad at their feet when walking out the back door on a summer evening. (Your back porch light attracts flying insects and the toad is taking advantage of the easy pickings.) Trying to get close to a frog before it jumps away is a fun activity for most kids.

Other people may enjoy the chorus of frogs calling from a small pool, ditch, pond or lake, or are happy to find an amphibian or reptile in their gardens, knowing it will eat garden pests. Some hunters actively seek out these creatures for food (five species are game animals in Missouri). Many students observe them for nature studies or scout badges. For years, farmers have welcomed the sight of black ratsnakes in their barns, knowing these harmless reptiles prey on rodents that would otherwise feast on valuable grain.

If left alone, most amphibians and reptiles will leave us alone. They will continue to enrich our lives with their songs, behaviors and their important roles in the natural world.

You can enjoy amphibians and reptiles close to home and help these amazing animals thrive by creating backyard habitat, such as this woodpile.

How Amphibians and Reptiles Live

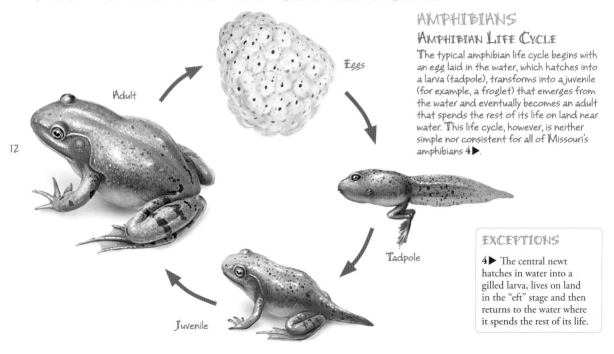

Adult

Eggs

Tadpole

Juvenile

12

Amphibian Life Cycle

The typical amphibian life cycle begins with an egg laid in the water, which hatches into a larva (tadpole), transforms into a juvenile (for example, a froglet) that emerges from the water and eventually becomes an adult that spends the rest of its life on land near water. This life cycle, however, is neither simple nor consistent for all of Missouri's amphibians 4▶.

EXCEPTIONS

4▶ The central newt hatches in water into a gilled larva, lives on land in the "eft" stage and then returns to the water where it spends the rest of its life.

Eggs

At first glance all amphibian eggs look alike. They are usually dark in the center with a clear or milky jelly-like coating. Most of what you see, however, did not come out of the mother. When the female lays the tiny dark eggs, they are covered only with a thin film. Once the eggs come in contact with water, the film absorbs water to create the protective jelly-like covering.

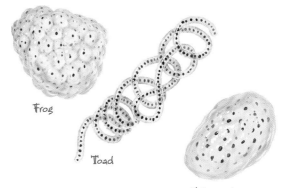

Frog

Toad

Salamander

13

There is an easy way to know if the eggs you find are from a toad, a frog or a salamander. Toads typically lay eggs in long strings, often in two strands attached to plants or sticks. Most frogs, on the other hand, lay eggs in a submerged, free-floating mass like a cluster of grapes. Even though the egg mass is a large grouping, you can distinguish one egg (complete with its jelly-like outer coating) from the one next to it. Several salamander species lay a mass that looks like one big clump of clear jelly with the eggs embedded into it **5▶**. Unless you look very closely, you would have a hard time seeing where the jelly of one egg ends and the jelly of the next egg begins.

COOL FACT: Some species of algae grow only on amphibian eggs. The algae provide oxygen to the developing eggs while the eggs give the algae a place to grow.

> ### EXCEPTIONS
>
> **5▶** Unlike the eggs of some other salamanders, hellbender eggs are connected like a strand of pearls. This extremely long strand is difficult to see in the large mass.

Most female amphibians lay one clutch of eggs every year. Different species lay different numbers of eggs, however. For example, spring peepers can produce several hundred eggs, laying them individually or in small clumps. The hellbender can lay between 200 and 700 eggs under large flat rocks in clear Ozark streams. Missouri's two most productive amphibians are the American bullfrog and Woodhouse's toad. A female bullfrog can lay more than 20,000 eggs in a summer clutch and a single female Woodhouse's toad can lay up to 25,000 eggs!

Small pools of water like this may not seem like good habitat, but they are perfect for amphibians. Because they dry up in the summertime, fish can't live in them. Without fish to prey on them, amphibian eggs have a better chance of hatching into larvae and growing up into adults.

JOHN MILLER

From Egg to Adult

Egg development varies among amphibians. Eggs of some, such as spring peepers, hatch in as few as three or four days, while hellbender eggs can take up to 35 days. Missouri toads and frogs do not stay with their eggs after they are laid—the eggs usually have enough water in the pool, pond or creek where they were laid to hatch and transform into juveniles that grow into adults.

Several salamanders, on the other hand, stay with their eggs until they hatch. With most of the lungless salamanders (long-tailed, cave and slimy), it's the female who cares for the eggs. With hellbenders, the male guards the eggs until they hatch. Parents of mole salamanders (tiger, spotted, mole, small-mouthed and ringed) do not stay with their eggs. Many amphibians return to the same bodies of water year after year to lay their eggs.

After hatching, an amphibian is usually called a larva (a frog larva is a tadpole or a polliwog). Depending on the species, a larva can take a few weeks to more than a year to transform and grow into an adult **6▶**.

Early on, most amphibian larvae look alike except for two major differences: gills and legs. All larval amphibians have gills to breathe oxygen from water. Salamander larvae have red or pink feathery gills that are easily seen sticking out of the neck. As most salamanders develop, they absorb their gills. The gills of toad and frog larvae are covered by a flap of skin around the neck, so they are not visible.

> **EXCEPTION**
>
> **6▶** American bullfrog tadpoles can take three to four years to become adults. This includes 11 to 14 months as tadpoles plus an additional two to three years to become adults.

Frogs and toads hatch with no legs. Typically, their back legs emerge first and the front legs second. If you get the chance to see the later development of a bullfrog tadpole, look carefully for the front legs. They actually develop under the skin near the gill cover. You can see the tiny legs moving under the skin as they work hard to punch through the skin.

Some salamanders, on the other hand, emerge from the egg with at least two tiny front legs. The back legs emerge later.

The presence or absence of a tail also helps distinguish an amphibian as a salamander or frog/toad. For a salamander, there is little change in the tail during the final transformation into an adult. Toad and frog tadpoles have tails, but not the adults. Contrary to popular belief, their tails do not "fall off." Rather they are absorbed into the body (getting shorter as the tadpole becomes a juvenile). When the juvenile—called a froglet or toadlet—emerges on land, it may briefly have a tiny tail. In a short span of time, the tail will be completely absorbed.

WHAT AMPHIBIANS EAT
As larvae, toads and frogs are primarily vegetarians, grazing like underwater cattle on algae and other soft plant material. Salamander larvae, on the other hand, are carnivores. As adults, all toads, frogs and salamanders are carnivores that eat smaller animals such as insects, spiders, worms and occasionally small fish and other amphibians.

REPTILES

FROM EGG OR BIRTH TO ADULT

All Missouri turtles and lizards lay eggs. The eggs are usually round or oval depending on the species and are covered with a pliable leathery shell. Female lizards usually lay their eggs in soft ground, in rotting logs or in piles of mulch. Some female lizards stay with a clutch of eggs until they hatch. Turtles lay eggs in the ground. They neither stay with the eggs nor help them hatch. Some of our Missouri turtles and lizards lay as few as two to seven eggs, such as the little brown skink, or as many as 52 eggs for the alligator snapping turtle. Hatching can take one and a half to three months.

JEFF BRIGGLER

A western painted turtle hatchling emerges from the ground where its mother laid her eggs.

COOL FACT: The position of a turtle egg in an underground nest will often determine the gender of the turtle. The warmer eggs on the top of the nest tend to become females while the eggs on the cooler bottom usually become males.

Of Missouri's 40 species of snakes, approximately half lay eggs (oviparous snakes) and the remaining half have live young (ovoviviparous snakes). Examples of egg-laying snakes include most of our larger snakes, such as ratsnakes, kingsnakes and the bullsnake. The flat-headed snake has the fewest number of eggs per clutch (one to four eggs), while the eastern hog-nosed snake can lay up to 61 eggs at a time. Snakes develop and hatch from eggs usually within two to three months of being laid. Egg-laying snakes usually do not stay with eggs as they develop.

Examples of snakes bearing live young include all five of our venomous snakes and all watersnakes, gartersnakes, ribbonsnakes and earthsnakes. While most live-bearing snakes have only a dozen or more snakes born at a time, the eastern gartersnake can have as many as 85 young in a litter.

Once born, all Missouri reptiles are like miniature versions of the adults. Some young reptiles, however, have slightly different coloration or patterns than adults to help them hide or escape predation. For the most part, young reptiles are much easier to identify than larval amphibians.

What Reptiles Eat

Most reptiles eat only other live animals, but turtles are omnivores, meaning they eat both plants and animals.

BEHAVIOR AND SURVIVAL

AVOIDING PREDATORS

Most amphibians and reptiles are predators, but they are also prey for animals such as hawks, owls, roadrunners, coyotes, raccoons and fish. Therefore, many amphibians and reptiles have green, brown, black or tan coloration to blend in with their surroundings, making it hard for predators to find them. It is also in these animals' best interest to venture out into the open only to find food, bask, breed or escape.

Because amphibians and reptiles are often out of sight, when we do see them they can startle or even frighten us. We often don't see them until we lift up a board or rock, move some leaves or weed the garden. For the most part, amphibians and reptiles will dart or slither away from us or other animals as quickly as possible. A few species, however, have developed some interesting adaptations to scare off intruders or predators.

JOHN MILLER

The eastern hog-nosed snake is a great actor: it fools predators with a dramatic, but harmless, bluff.

One of these is the eastern hog-nosed snake. If it feels it is being threatened, it will carry out an elaborate bluff. This behavior includes inflating its body like a tire inner tube, flattening its head like a cobra (which does not live in North America) and making nasal hissing noises. The snake is indeed trying to scare you into leaving it alone. If all else fails and the hog-nosed snake perceives it is in danger, it has one last trick—it plays dead. At some point the hog-nosed snake begins to writhe as if in death throes. It will throw up, release feces (poop) and hang out its tongue. Finally, it will roll over on its back and remain motionless. After you leave (or back away a short distance) the snake will slowly right itself on its belly and slither away.

Other snakes you encounter may not immediately distance themselves from you; they stay put, hoping their coloration will keep them from view. One Missouri snake whose coloration is not camouflaged with its background is the red milksnake. Though it is nonvenomous and harmless to people, its vivid red color serves as a "warning: danger" sign to other animals—this is one of the tricks of the natural world!

COOL FACT: Even though only five of Missouri's 40 species of snakes are venomous, the best advice when encountering any snake is "leave it alone." Although the snake may be harmless to you, *you* may distress the animal or cause it to defend itself.

SURVIVING HEAT AND COLD

Extreme hot and cold temperatures can be challenging for herps. Unlike "endothermic" mammals and birds, which can regulate body temperature internally, herps are "ectothermic," meaning they must rely on their environment to stay cool or warm.

Most Missouri herps are active between the temperatures of 60° to 85° F. When temperatures become cooler, they become less active and must seek warmer places (sunlight, rocks or water) to warm up. Except for a few frog and turtle species, freezing temperatures can kill herps. To survive cold weather, herps overwinter below the frost line underground or deep in the water. Because "hibernation" is a complex strategy used mainly by mammals, most herpetologists use the terms "overwintering" or "brumation" to describe how herps make it through the coldest times of the year.

Warm temperatures help a herp increase its body temperature and activity, but hot temperatures are often lethal. In the heat of a summer day, many herps seek shelter from the sun or wait until nightfall when temperatures are more favorable. To survive hot periods, many herps will move to cooler locations, such as under rocks or in water. Many also become nocturnal in hot weather.

By moving from cooler or warmer locations throughout the day and night, a herp can keep its body temperature stable, even though daily temperatures may change by as much as 30° F. Healthy habitats greatly improve a herp's ability to survive extremes of heat or cold.

Catch, Study and Release

Observing and photographing herps is the best way to learn about these animals. Collecting should be done under adult supervision and only when it is allowed.

THE WILDLIFE CODE OF MISSOURI

The Wildlife Code of Missouri is a set of regulations intended to manage Missouri's valuable plant and animal communities, to provide equal opportunity to share and enjoy these resources and to promote public safety. According to the Wildlife Code, all amphibians and reptiles—except for the bullfrog, green frog, eastern snapping turtle and softshell turtles—are protected as non-game species. This gives them protection from unnecessary harassment or destruction. This also means that amphibians and reptiles caught in Missouri cannot be sold in stores or taken out of the state unless proper permits have been obtained.

The Wildlife Code does, however, give all Missourians the opportunity to temporarily possess up to five amphibians or reptiles for personal study 7▶. Whenever possible, it is best to look on your own property for herps so you don't have to ask permission and so you can easily release the animals back where you found them.

EXCEPTION

7▶ Exceptions are all venomous snakes, the dusty hog-nosed snake, the Kirtland's snake, the western foxsnake, the alligator snapping turtle and endangered herps. Check with your local Missouri Department of Conservation office for a current listing of endangered species in the state.

MDC

GET PERMISSION BEFORE COLLECTING

If you want to look for herps beyond your own property, you must first find out where it is legal to collect. Remember that most public areas like state parks, conservation areas, national forests or county parks do not allow animal collecting. In most cases you will be allowed to look and take photos, but you should always ask the park or area manager about site regulations on catching or looking for amphibians and reptiles. If catching these animals is allowed, it is always best to release them after you photograph them so that others can enjoy them too. Because 93 percent of Missouri is owned by private citizens, there are many herping opportunities around you besides going on public property. If you intend to go to a neighbor's property, always ask for permission first.

With just a net and a bucket, you can have fun catching and observing amphibians and reptiles. Make sure to read the information on these and the following pages to help, and not harm, these wonderful creatures.

HELP STOP THE AMPHIBIAN CHYTRID FUNGUS

Even if you are not collecting and just observing, be aware of transporting the amphibian chytrid (pronounced *kit-trid*) fungus from water body to water body. The amphibian chytrid fungus is an invasive species from Africa that can live on amphibians and harm or kill them. This fungus is already affecting some Missouri species. It also has been linked to the extinction of several amphibian species around the world. If you are looking for amphibians or reptiles in the water, you should not go from pond to pond without either disinfecting your boots and equipment with bleach at home or using different equipment for each pond. *Always* return an animal to the pond, creek or river where you found it. Otherwise, you could be spreading this fungus to new places, harming the animals that you enjoy.

TAKING CARE OF AMPHIBIANS AND REPTILES

If you decide that you would like to keep a herp for a few days, you need to know how to take care of it so you can release it in the same health as when you caught it. Do your research *before* collecting to make sure you can transport, house, feed, water and protect the herp properly. Care information for many amphibians and reptiles is available from the Missouri Department of Conservation, local herpetological societies and reputable pet stores.

RELEASING HEALTHY HERPS

If you do collect a herp, you should make every effort to return it back to the location where you found it. If you found a salamander near a spring at your neighbor's property, you should take it back to that very spring. Letting it go in your backyard may not be the correct habitat. If you found a box turtle while driving along a country road, you should return the turtle to a safe spot along the same country road. It is not advisable to collect an animal while on vacation as you will probably not be able to care for it properly while away from home, and you may live far from your vacation spot, making it impossible for you to return the animal where you found it. For those reasons you should collect only from areas near your home.

When releasing an animal, make sure it has time to overwinter. You should release the healthy herp back into the wild in plenty of time for it to prepare for winter survival. Avoid keeping the animal for more than one or two months at the most. The sooner you release the animal where you found it, the better its chances of survival. Animals kept in captivity for six months or longer may lose the ability to return to the wild. Collecting an animal in September and releasing it in November gives it no time to properly prepare for winter survival—so don't collect after August. Never, ever collect amphibians and reptiles from other states or countries and release them into Missouri. That is biologically dangerous and illegal. It also is illegal to release herps into the wild that were purchased on-line or from pet stores, even if they are native species.

Rules for Field Study

• Making observations and taking photographs are better for herps than collecting them. If you do collect, however, follow the guidance on the previous pages.

• If you go "herping," stay off private property unless you have permission to be there. If you are on public land, you should understand rules for exploring sensitive areas, walking off trails, moving animals to photograph them or turning over rocks or logs to find herps. Each area or park may have different regulations—it is your responsibility to ask the area or park manager what is permissible.

• Be a good herping role model. If you collect an amphibian or a reptile, you should not only release it unharmed and in its original location, but you should also leave the area better than you found it. Pick up all trash you find and let the area manager know if you noticed habitat damage or litter. Always return a rock or log to its original location. Put the rock or log back exactly as it was, then release the herp so it can find its way back to its hiding place on its own. While a rock may look like "any old rock," it is a vital habitat component that may be the only place an amphibian or reptile has to hide, lay eggs, find food or find water. By taking care of herp habitats and not harming animals, there will be opportunities for field study for generations to come.

AMPHIBIAN AND REPTILE GAME SPECIES

Eastern Snapping Turtle

Spiny Softshell Turtle

Midland Smooth Softshell Turtle

Bullfrog

Green Frog

PHOTOS MDC

The herps pictured here are game species.
To harvest these animals, you need a Missouri
hunting or fishing permit. Consult the
Missouri Department of Conservation's
fishing regulations for details.

CONSERVATION

Conservation is the careful protection and management of land, air, soil, water, animals and plants. Conservation is the key to amphibian and reptile survival. Herps live in every type of natural community in Missouri—forests, woodlands, glades, prairies, wetlands and streams. Conservation involves all of us working together to protect these habitats; reducing water, air and soil pollution; and helping stop the spread of the amphibian chytrid fungus. Conservation also means preventing herps from being exploited by collectors who are capturing them illegally for the pet trade. With conservation, we can continue to study and enjoy these animals in their natural habitats.

HERPS HELP US!

In many cases, seeing a variety of amphibians and reptiles is a sign of clean water and healthy habitats—two things people need as well. Having stable amphibian and reptile habitats also provides food, water and shelter for other groups of animals such as mammals, birds and fish—other creatures we also enjoy in Missouri.

Because amphibians and reptiles are sensitive to changes in their surroundings, they are good indicators of habitat threats. A good example is the hellbender, Missouri's largest salamander. Some of our cleanest cold streams used to have hundreds of hellbenders. Today we are lucky to find just a few individuals in the same streams. By understanding what is affecting the hellbenders we may be able to prevent other animals from declining in these Ozark streams.

Understanding our amphibians and reptiles gives us more reason to appreciate our diverse state and conserve the resources we all share.

WHAT CAN YOU DO TO HELP CONSERVE HERPS?

- Use **Show-Me Herps** to learn about these amazing creatures and what they need to survive.
- Participate in volunteer programs such as the Missouri Stream Team or the Frog and Toad Calling Survey to help biologists monitor habitat health and population numbers. For more information on the Stream Team visit www.MoStreamTeam.org or call 800-781-1989; for the Frog and Toad Calling Survey, call the Missouri Department of Conservation at 573-522-4115.
- Always release herps to the same place you found them. This helps herps survive and also prevents the amphibian chytrid fungus from spreading to new places.
- If you handle amphibians, make sure your hands are clean, with no insect repellent or lotion on your skin. These substances were not meant for amphibian skin.
- Discourage your friends and family members from buying animals caught from the wild, from Missouri or elsewhere. Sadly, some unethical individuals continue to collect herps illegally for the pet trade, often removing all animals from a location and destroying the habitat in the process. If people don't buy illegally collected herps, illegal collectors will stop collecting.
- Conserve or restore the habitats that herps need. Reptiles such as eastern collared lizards and milksnakes need sunny glades. Removing encroaching cedars on glades will help these animals. Many amphibians need shallow pools without fish, so their eggs and tadpoles won't be eaten. Creating pools that fill with water in spring, but dry up in the summer, are perfect for amphibian breeding.
- Protect remaining prairies, forests, woodlands, wetlands, glades and streams to ensure that all of Missouri's herps will live in the state for generations to come.

How to Use this Book

This book includes 18 amphibians and 32 reptiles that live in Missouri. Amphibians are grouped first, followed by reptiles.

Toad and frog measurements are given from "snout to vent." The vent is the rear end of the animal. The legs are not counted in the measurements. Salamanders, lizards and snakes are measured from the tip of the nose to the end of the tail. Turtles are measured from the front of the top shell (carapace) to the back in a straight line.

Both common and scientific names are given for each animal. Names provided are the most updated versions. Most people use common names to identify amphibians and reptiles they see. The scientific name is usually two words. The first is called the genus name and the second the species name. For some herps, there is a third name or subspecies. Subspecies names are used for herps that are very closely related, but have subtle differences, such as *Graptemys pseudogeographica pseudogeographica* (false map turtle) and *Graptemys pseudogeographica kohnii* (Mississippi

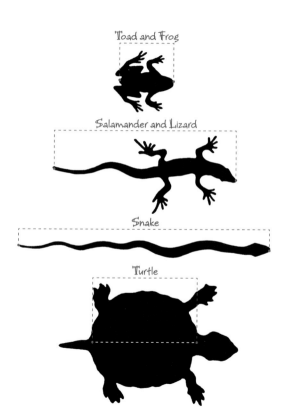

Toad and Frog

Salamander and Lizard

Snake

Turtle

map turtle). Scientific names are recognized around the world and help scientists avoid confusion over common names. One good example is the "puff adder." The harmless "puff adder" (eastern hog-nosed snake) of North America is *Heterodon platirhinos* while the dangerous "puff adder" of Africa is *Bitis arietans*. Knowing the scientific name could save your life!

Physical descriptions are provided in the text to accompany the richly colored and detailed illustrations. Most of the herps pictured are adults. Young of the same species may look different, and males and females can differ in appearance as well. The text provides information about some of these differences. You also may want to use a reference listed on page 148 to identify a juvenile herp.

General range and habitat descriptions are given for each animal in the "Habitat and Food" section. Some herps live throughout Missouri, while others are found only in a particular region of the state. Some herps eat a wide variety of food and others prey only on specific animals. Knowing where and how a herp lives may help you identify one you see in the wild.

For a complete guide to all amphibians and reptiles in Missouri, check out Tom R. Johnson's *The Amphibians and Reptiles of Missouri* book, published by the Missouri Department of Conservation. Johnson's book is the basis of knowledge for the work of many herpetologists, as well as for Show-Me Herps. *The Amphibians and Reptiles of Missouri* provides detailed information on all species of herps in Missouri, including range maps for each animal. See page 148 for ordering information.

PART TWO: 18 AMAZING AMPHIBIANS IN MISSOURI

33

Hellbender

SPECIES:
Cryptobranchus alleganiensis

This strange-looking, but harmless, amphibian is Missouri's largest salamander. It is a muddy brown color and has a flat wide head and tiny eyes. Hellbenders have no external gills as adults. Wavy folds of skin along their sides help them absorb oxygen from the water.

HABITAT AND FOOD:

Hellbenders spend their entire lives in the cold, clear waters of our larger Ozark streams. They feed mainly on crayfish.

COOL FACTS:

- Missouri is the only state to have two types of hellbenders, the Ozark hellbender and the eastern hellbender.
- Hellbenders are long-lived animals and may live up to 40 years.
- The name "hellbender" probably comes from settlers seeing the animal's odd looks and thinking "it was a creature from hell where it's bent on returning."

Both subspecies of hellbender (eastern and Ozark) are endangered in Missouri. Their decline in the state may be due to water pollution and stream disturbance in Ozark streams, and because of illegal collection. If you should accidentally catch a hellbender while fishing, release it unharmed.

11 to 24 inches long

Mudpuppy

SPECIES:
Necturus maculosus

The mudpuppy is totally aquatic its entire life. It has a slender brown-to-gray body with irregular spots and feathery pink or red gills sticking out of its neck. It has a relatively flat head and tiny eyes. Although both larvae and adults retain gills, adults lack the long heavy stripes found on the larvae.

HABITAT AND FOOD:

Mudpuppies live in permanent bodies of water such as lakes and large creeks and rivers, including the Mississippi and Missouri. They live throughout the state except in northwestern and north-central Missouri. Mudpuppies are not easy to find. They tend to remain hidden under rocks and logs until night when they hunt for food. They eat just about any aquatic animals they can swallow; this includes crayfish, small mussels, small fish, aquatic worms and aquatic insects.

COOL FACTS:

- Mudpuppies can live for 20 years or more.
- Mudpuppies are the only known hosts for larvae of the imperiled salamander mussel.

8 to 16½ inches long

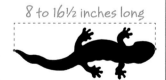

Unlike hellbenders, adult mudpuppies retain external gills. They reproduce in what appears to be the larval stage (neotenic).

Central Newt

SPECIES:
Notophthalmus viridescens louisianensis

This olive-green salamander with a yellow belly has a dark stripe running from the nose through the eye to the neck. It has small black spots along the back and sides; some individuals also have tiny red spots.

HABITAT AND FOOD:

Central newts are found across most of the state except northwestern Missouri. Adults live primarily in woodland ponds, swamps and occasionally water-filled ditches. Newts in the juvenile "eft" stage can be found under rocks and logs in wooded areas near fishless ponds. They eat a variety of small invertebrates as well as small salamanders and tadpoles.

COOL FACT:

• Newts have toxic skin to protect them from predators.

2½ to 4 inches long

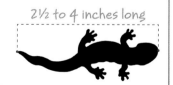

Newts have an extra life stage, called an "eft," that most salamanders don't have. A newt begins its life in the water as an egg and hatches into a larva. Emerging onto land, it becomes a reddish brown eft. It can spend two to three years on land before returning to water, where it turns olive-green and lives the rest of its life as an aquatic adult.

39

Ringed Salamander

SPECIES:
Ambystoma annulatum

Approximately 10 to 15 light yellow rings across the top of this dark salamander make it easy to identify. The belly is light gray.

HABITAT AND FOOD:

Ringed salamanders live in heavily forested areas and prefer to stay hidden below rocks and logs. They are found in a wide diagonal area from St. Louis to Branson and the southern Ozarks. They are rarely found elsewhere in the state. Ringed salamanders most likely eat earthworms, insects and snails.

COOL FACTS:

- Because they spend so much time underground, ringed salamanders are in a group called "mole salamanders." There are five other species of mole salamanders in Missouri—tiger, spotted, marbled, mole and small-mouthed.
- Ringed salamanders breed in the fall, especially after rains.
- Their eggs hatch in the early fall, and larvae survive over the winter.

5 to 9½ inches long

Many salamanders can be identified by the number of "costal grooves" or vertical indentations they have on their sides between their front and back legs. The ringed salamander usually has 15 costal grooves.

Spotted Salamander

SPECIES: *Ambystoma maculatum*	Spotted salamanders are slate black with irregular rows of distinct spots. Head spots are typically orange and the rest on the body and tail are yellow. The belly is dark gray. Spotted salamanders may have 11 to 12 costal grooves between the front and back legs.
HABITAT AND FOOD:	Spotted salamanders are found in moist hardwood forests and near fishless ponds. They are common across most forested areas of southern Missouri except for the Bootheel. They hide under dead leaves, rocks and logs. They feed at night on worms, insects, land snails and spiders.
COOL FACTS:	• One female can lay three or four egg masses, each containing 12 to 250 eggs. • The distribution of the spotted salamander in the United States is nearly identical to that of the short-tailed shrew. • Large numbers of spotted salamanders may cross country roads on rainy evenings.

42

6 to 8½ inches long

A species of algae grows on the jelly-like mass surrounding the eggs of this salamander. The algae provide oxygen to the eggs and the mass provides carbon dioxide and nutrients to the algae.

Western Slimy Salamander

SPECIES:
Plethodon albagula

Snowflakes seem to adorn the back of this medium-sized salamander. It is black on top with tiny random and irregular silver patches from head to tail. The belly and chin are dark gray. Slimy salamanders typically have 16 costal grooves.

HABITAT AND FOOD:

Western slimy salamanders are found under logs and rocks in moist forested hillsides of the Ozarks (but not in the Bootheel or prairie regions). They feed primarily on small beetles and ants.

COOL FACTS:

- Western slimy salamanders have no larval stage. Eggs are laid not in water, but under rotten logs or in caves. They hatch into miniature adults.
- These salamanders release sticky secretions that are difficult to remove from your fingers and hands.
- Like snakes, salamanders periodically shed their skins.

4¾ to 8 inches long

Western slimy salamanders belong to a group called "lungless salamanders"—they don't have lungs and most don't have gills. They absorb oxygen through their skins and the mucous membranes in their mouths.

45

Long-tailed Salamander

SPECIES:
Eurycea longicauda

Aptly named, this medium-sized salamander has a tail that is longer than the rest of its body. It is yellow to orange-yellow with dark spots or patches along the top and sides of its body. It has dark vertical bars on the sides of the tail and 13 to 14 costal grooves.

HABITAT AND FOOD:

These salamanders are common across the Ozark highlands, but are rarely found elsewhere in Missouri. They live mainly in forested areas near springs, streams and seeps on hillsides. They also are occasionally found in caves. Long-tailed salamanders eat primarily small arthropods.

COOL FACTS:

- This salamander is known to wave its tail to distract potential predators and attacks to its head.
- Like lizards and some other salamanders, a long-tailed salamander can break off its tail if grabbed.
- There are two subspecies of this salamander—one called the long-tailed and the other the dark-sided.

4 to 6 inches long

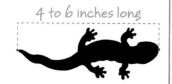

Forest owners can help these salamanders by letting rotten logs lie on the forest floor, which long-tailed and other lungless salamanders can use for shelter.

Cave Salamander

SPECIES:
Eurycea lucifuga

This medium-sized, thin salamander is bright orange-red on top with random tiny black spots. The lighter belly has no spots. The tail is often as long or longer than the body. The cave salamander has 13 to 14 costal grooves on its sides.

HABITAT AND FOOD:

As the name implies, these salamanders live in or near caves. They also can be found along moist limestone outcrops, as well as in wooded and rocky areas along streams and springs. Cave salamanders live across most of the Ozarks, but are absent from the Bootheel. They eat small cave arthropods.

COOL FACTS:

- The cave salamander is an excellent climber and can be found on cave walls, stalactites and stalagmites.
- It will wave its tail to distract a potential predator.
- Females lay eggs in streams, pools in caves and small streams.

4 to 7 inches long

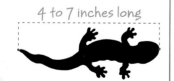

Cave salamanders may be the largest predators living in a small cave. Leaving them alone will protect the food chain of a cave habitat.

49

American Toad

SPECIES:
Anaxyrus americanus

This medium-sized toad can be dark brown, light brown or even reddish orange. It has a large bean-shaped bump (parotoid gland) behind each eye. The two circles (one behind each eye) are external eardrums called tympanums. Dark spots on the back may contain one to three small bumps.

HABITAT AND FOOD:

American toads are common across the state in cities and in the countryside. They live in rocky woodlands and along the edge of hardwood forests, but also are commonly found in backyards, gardens and small burrows. This species, like many other toads, eats worms and insects at night.

COOL FACTS:

- Toads don't give people warts—this is a myth.
- Females can lay as many as 20,000 eggs in long double strands that look like strings of black pearls.
- You can imitate the call of the male American toad by vibrating your lips and humming in a high pitch.

2 to 4 inches long

Toads protect themselves from predators not by speed, claws or teeth, but by poisonous skin! Bumps on a toad's skin produce a foul-tasting substance that most animals find inedible.

Eastern Narrow-mouthed Toad

SPECIES:
Gastrophryne carolinensis

This small pudgy toad can be brown, reddish brown or tan. Its skin is smoother and slimier than other true toads (members of the genus *Anaxyrus*). It has a pointed nose and a fold of skin across the head just behind the eyes.

HABITAT AND FOOD:

Eastern narrow-mouthed toads are common across southern Missouri, but are rarely found north of the Missouri River or in extreme western Missouri. They live in moist forests of the Ozarks close to streams, ponds and swamps. They spend most of the time in loose soil, leaf litter or below rocks and logs. These toads eat almost exclusively ants, but they also can eat termites and small beetles.

COOL FACTS:

- The males' call sounds like a lost sheep—a nasal, bleating *baaaa*.
- During breeding, the male produces a sticky substance that helps "glue" him to his mate.

1 to 1½ inches long

The eastern narrow-mouthed toad can push the fold of skin on its head forward to cover its eyes while eating ants. This protects its eyes from ant bites.

53

Northern Cricket Frog

(formerly called Blanchard's Cricket Frog)

SPECIES:
Acris crepitans

If you see a small, light-to-dark brown frog on a gravel bar, chances are it is a northern cricket frog. Look for a dark triangle between the eyes that points toward the back. The cricket frog may have an irregular stripe on its back that can be green, rusty red or brown.

HABITAT AND FOOD:

Northern cricket frogs are common across the state. They are found mainly in open areas along streams, ponds, lakes and even in water-filled ditches in the middle of a town. They eat mainly terrestrial insects.

COOL FACTS:

• When approached, cricket frogs will jump into the water but will quickly return to shore.

• A cricket frog tadpole may use its black-tipped tail to avoid capture by predators: the tail breaks off easily, allowing the tadpole to escape. Sometimes the tail will grow back.

½ to 1½ inches long

The name of this frog comes from the males' call, which to some people sounds like a cricket. You can imitate this sound by taking two smooth round rocks and striking them together with a progressively faster speed.

Green Treefrog

SPECIES:
Hyla cinerea

This medium-sized frog is solid lime green with tiny gold spots scattered on its back. A white stripe extends from the upper lip to the sides of the body. The belly and inside of the legs are light colored.

HABITAT AND FOOD:

In our state, these amphibians are common only in the Bootheel and aren't found outside of this region except for a small, introduced population near the Lake of the Ozarks. Green treefrogs live mostly in bottomlands, swamps and marshes. Their green camouflage allows them to spend much of their days resting undetected among plants. At night, they hunt for insects.

COOL FACTS:

- This is one of only three true treefrogs in the state. The other two are the gray treefrog and Cope's gray treefrog.
- Like most treefrogs, green treefrogs have toe pads to help them climb on vegetation.

1¼ to 2¼ inches long

The nasal *guank, guank* call of the green treefrog sounds like a duck. A chorus of green treefrogs can sound like Canada geese calling in the distance.

57

Gray Treefrog

SPECIES:
Hyla versicolor

This medium-sized frog has sticky, bumpy skin that can range from gray to lime green. Regardless of color, there is a white patch below each eye and an irregular, dark marking in the center of the back. It has bright orange patches on the inside of the hind legs. Toe pads help this frog climb many different surfaces.

HABITAT AND FOOD:

Gray treefrogs are common and live statewide in forests, trees along prairie streams, bottomland forests, rivers and swamps. Adults spend most of their lives in vegetation, but go into water to breed. Gray treefrogs eat insects, spiders and other small invertebrates.

COOL FACTS:

- A gray treefrog can change color from gray to lime green. This helps it blend into a variety of backgrounds.
- Cope's gray treefrog is almost identical in appearance to the gray treefrog, but its call is nearly twice as fast.

1¼ to 2 inches long

Like several other frog species in Missouri, gray treefrogs produce a type of blood "antifreeze" that keeps them from freezing in the winter.

59

Spring Peeper

SPECIES:
Pseudacris crucifer

With a distinctive X on its back, this small light-to-dark brown frog is fairly easy to identify. It also has a dark line on top of its head between the eyes and several dark bars on the legs. Its toe pads allow it to climb on vegetation.

HABITAT AND FOOD:

Spring peepers are common across Missouri except for the extreme northwestern corner of the state. They live along streams, ponds and woodland swamps. Peepers prefer to breed in fishless ponds. They eat a variety of spiders and small insects.

COOL FACTS:

- Peepers are one of the earliest frogs to call in the spring.
- Some individuals can be heard in the fall.
- Eggs hatch in as little as three to four days and can transform into juveniles in about two months.

3/4 to 1¼ inches long

The male spring peeper's call is a repeating, short, lilting *peep*, which also sounds like a quick whistle that you might use to call a dog. When these small frogs mass together at a pond, the sound can be nearly deafening.

Boreal Chorus Frog (formerly called Western Chorus Frog)

SPECIES: *Pseudacris maculata*	This small gray or light brown frog has three stripes running down its back. The stripes may be continuous or broken. It also has a wide dark stripe extending from the nose, through the eye and ending at the hips. The upper lip is usually white.
HABITAT AND FOOD:	Boreal chorus frogs are common across Missouri except for the Bootheel. They live in prairies and other open habitats such as marshes, river floodplains and along crop fields. Boreal chorus frogs eat spiders and small insects.
COOL FACTS:	• Boreal chorus frogs can tolerate freezing temperatures by increasing the glucose level in their blood. • During the breeding season, the male's throat looks dark because capillaries are supplying blood to the vocal sac.

62

¾ to 1½ inches long

The call of the male boreal chorus frog can be described as a vibrating *prrreeep.* You can imitate this sound if you run your thumb down the teeth of a large plastic comb. Chorus frogs inflate their vocal sacs to resonate and amplify their calls, which are produced deep in the throat.

63

American Bullfrog

SPECIES:
Lithobates catesbeianus

This is Missouri's largest frog. Its skin is covered with tiny bumps and can be dark green, light green or bronze. The upper lip is usually green. The legs have distinct dark brown bars.

HABITAT AND FOOD:

American bullfrogs are common throughout the state. They live in ponds, lakes, swamps and streams. They are voracious carnivores. Bullfrogs eat live food including earthworms, insects, small fish, other frogs and even small birds—if one is slow enough.

COOL FACTS:

- The American bullfrog became Missouri's state amphibian in 2005.
- Bullfrogs are one of two game frogs in Missouri. Many people think that bullfrog legs are quite delicious.
- Because of its size and appetite, a bullfrog can outcompete other amphibians.
- The low, slow, deep *gerr-ger-rum, gerr-ger-rum* song of the male bullfrog is one of summer's welcome night sounds.

3 to 6¾ inches long

Bullfrogs can take up to two years to develop from egg to froglet. In the winter, you might see bullfrog tadpoles under the ice of a pond or lake. They are waiting for the next summer to make their final transformation into juveniles and then adults.

Green Frog

SPECIES:
Lithobates clamitans

This large green-to-brown frog has rough slimy skin and looks a lot like the American bullfrog. To tell the two apart, look at the raised fold of skin that both frogs have behind each eye. On bullfrogs the fold curves down to the armpit, but on green frogs the fold extends down the side of the back.

HABITAT AND FOOD:

Green frogs are common across most of the state except for the extreme northwestern corner. They live in streams, rivers, farm ponds, sloughs, swamps and marshes, where they prey on small crayfish and insects.

COOL FACTS:

- The call of the male green frog is an explosive *bong* that sounds like a loose banjo string.
- Like bullfrogs, the green frog is a game species.

2 to 3½ inches long

You can tell male and female green frogs (and bullfrogs) apart by comparing the size of the eye and the tympanum (ear drum) behind the eye. If they are similar in size, the frog is a female. If the tympanum is larger than the eye, the frog is a male.

67

Southern Leopard Frog

SPECIES:
Lithobates sphenocephalus

Like a leopard, this medium-sized frog has large, random, round or oblong spots down its back and legs. Its back can be vivid green or brown and its belly is white. The southern leopard frog has a white or yellow raised fold of skin along each side of the back from eye to groin. This frog is sometimes confused with the pickerel frog.

HABITAT AND FOOD:

Southern leopard frogs are common across the state except for extreme northwestern Missouri. They live in flooded ditches, ponds, sloughs, streams and lakes. They also can be found away from water in fields when searching for food. They eat a variety of insects and other invertebrates.

COOL FACTS:

• The other two leopard frogs in Missouri are the northern leopard frog and the plains leopard frog.
• All leopard frogs have two vocal sacs, one on each side of the throat.

2 to 3¼ inches long

The call of the male southern leopard frog is an explosive chuckle or cackle. It almost sounds like the leopard frog is laughing!

69

PART THREE: 32 REMARKABLE REPTILES IN MISSOURI

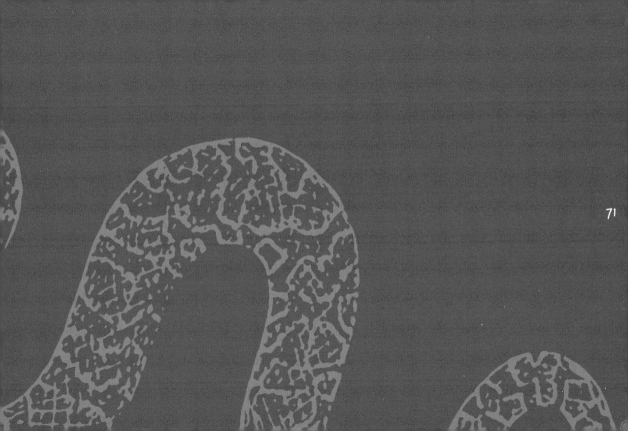

Eastern Snapping Turtle

(formerly called Common Snapping Turtle)

SPECIES:
Chelydra serpentina

This large aquatic turtle has a proportionately small pointed head that fits easily into its shell. The top shell (carapace) can be tan, brown or nearly black and has small or few raised ridges and three large rows of scales. The bottom shell (plastron) and legs are yellowish white. The spiked tail can be 10 inches or longer. Average weight is 10 to 35 pounds.

HABITAT AND FOOD:

Eastern snapping turtles are common and found in every county in Missouri. They live in ponds, lakes, streams, swamps, marshes and sloughs. Snapping turtles eat a variety of dead and living animals, such as fish, amphibians, insects and small mammals, and even aquatic vegetation.

COOL FACTS:

8 to 14½ inches long

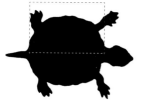

- The snapping turtle gets its name from its ability to rapidly bite and hold on to prey.
- These turtles will bite people only in defense—so putting fingers, toes or sticks near a snapping turtle's mouth is not a good idea!

Snapping turtles do not "clean out" ponds of fish. By eating slow and sick fish, they actually help fish populations remain healthy.

Alligator Snapping Turtle

SPECIES:
Macrochelys temminckii

This large dark brown aquatic turtle can weigh 35 to 150 pounds! It has a large head that looks oversized for its shell. The top shell (carapace) has distinctive ridges and five rows of scales. The bottom shell (plastron) and legs are dark or black. The top of the mouth has a sharp, raptor-like beak and the neck has spike-like projections. The long tail has small smooth bumps.

HABITAT AND FOOD:

74

Alligator snapping turtles are rare and found only in extreme southern Missouri, the Bootheel and occasionally along the Mississippi River. They live in large rivers, oxbow lakes and deep sloughs. They feed mainly on fish.

COOL FACTS:

15 to 16½ inches long

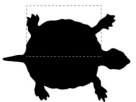

- Alligators snapping turtles rarely leave the water. If you see one on land, it may be a female looking for a place to lay her eggs.

- Like other aquatic turtles, alligator snapping turtles will bite to protect themselves if provoked.

- These are North America's largest freshwater turtles. The record weight for one is 316 pounds!

The alligator snapping turtle uses a pink worm-like tongue projection to catch fish. By wiggling its tongue, this turtle can sometimes lure unsuspecting fish into its awaiting jaws.

Western Painted Turtle

SPECIES:
Chrysemys picta bellii

Vivid orange-red patterns look as if they've been painted along the edge of the dark, smooth top shell (carapace) of this medium-sized, semi-aquatic turtle. The bottom shell (plaston) is yellow-orange, bright orange or red, and there are bright yellow (and sometimes red) lines on the face, neck and legs.

HABITAT AND FOOD:

Western painted turtles are found throughout Missouri, especially in the prairie regions. They live in marshes, lakes, slow-moving rivers, oxbow lakes and ponds with healthy aquatic vegetation. You can often see them basking in the sun on rocks, logs or thick vegetation. They quickly slide into water to escape. Western painted turtles are omnivores and feed on plants, snails, crayfish, insects and occasionally fish.

COOL FACTS:

- Western painted turtles live as far north as southern Canada.
- The southern painted turtle, which replaces the western painted turtle in the Bootheel, has a red or orange stripe down the center of its back and a light cream belly.

76

3 to 8 inches long

If eggs are laid late in the summer, newly hatched western painted turtles remain underground until the following spring when they emerge above ground.

Northern Map Turtle (formerly called Common Map Turtle)

SPECIES:
Graptemys geographica

A fine pattern of lines like those found on a topographic map covers the olive-brown top shell (carapace) of the northern map turtle, which is why its species name is *geographica*. This medium-sized, semi-aquatic turtle has a distinct yellow spot located behind each eye. Each spot may have one or two sharp points. Exposed skin is dark brown with narrow yellow stripes. The bottom shell (plastron) is a light cream color.

HABITAT AND FOOD:

Northern map turtles are common in the Ozarks to northeastern Missouri. Map turtles live in rivers, streams, oxbow lakes and sloughs with healthy aquatic vegetation. You can often see them basking in the sun on rocks, logs or thick mats of water plants. They quickly slide off to escape. Northern map turtles feed on mussels, snails, crayfish and some insects.

COOL FACTS:

7 to 8¾ inches long

- Map turtles' jaws are adapted to cracking the shells of mussels and snails.
- There are four types of map turtles in Missouri: the northern, Ouachita, Mississippi and false map turtles.

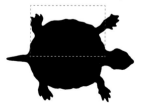

Map turtles can remain active in the winter. Herpetologists have even seen them swimming below ice in rivers!

False Map Turtle

SPECIES:
Graptemys pseudogeographica pseudogeographica

This medium-sized, semi-aquatic turtle has an olive-brown top shell (carapace) with two or three raised peaks and a jagged back edge. The bottom shell (plastron) is mostly cream-yellow with darker patterns at scale borders. Behind each eye is a distinctive yellow backward "L" marking. Legs are dark with yellow lines.

HABITAT AND FOOD:

False map turtles live mainly along stretches of the Missouri, Mississippi and Osage Rivers, including their channels, sloughs and oxbow lakes. These turtles feed on insects, worms, crayfish, snails, dead fish and some aquatic plants.

COOL FACT:

• Basking turtles, such as the false map turtle, sun themselves on rocks, logs or mats of vegetation to raise their body temperature and produce vitamin D.

5 to 6¼ inches long

This turtle is often mistaken for the northern map turtle and closely related Mississippi map turtle. You can tell them apart by the yellow marking behind the eye. The northern map turtle has a small yellow spot; the false map turtle has a backward "L" that points down the neck; the Mississippi map turtle has a crescent that faces forward.

Eastern River Cooter (formerly called River Cooter)

SPECIES:
Pseudemys concinna concinna

This medium-sized aquatic turtle has a broad top shell (carapace) that is olive-brown to nearly black and covered with yellow circular stripes that look like lines on a topographic map. The bottom shell (plastron) is solid light yellow and there is a distinct yellow "Y" marking on the head below the cheek and eye. The skin of the head, neck and legs is dark with several yellow lines.

HABITAT AND FOOD:

Cooters live south of the Missouri River in large lakes, rivers and sloughs. They spend much of the time basking on logs and rocks. They eat aquatic plants, but some herpetologists believe they also may eat mussels, crayfish and insects.

COOL FACTS:

- The eastern river cooter is one of Missouri's largest basking turtles.
- "Cooter" comes from the word *kuta*, which means "turtle" in several West African languages.
- An eastern river cooter can remain inactive and even sleep underwater during cold temperatures by slowing down its metabolism and absorbing oxygen through its cloaca.

9 to 13 inches long

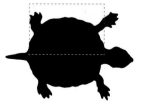

Like other basking turtles, you can tell an adult male eastern river cooter from a female by its long front claws and large, long tail.

83

Three-toed Box Turtle

SPECIES:
Terrapene carolina triunguis

Normally, the three-toed box turtle has three toes on its back feet, but some individuals can have four! This small land turtle has an olive-green or dark brown domed top shell (carapace) that is plain or marked with yellow streaks in random patterns. The center of the carapace usually has a raised ridge. The bottom shell (plastron) is plain or has faint markings.

HABITAT AND FOOD:

Three-toed box turtles are common across most of Missouri. They live in mature oak-hickory forests, forest borders and brushy fields. They bask in open areas to warm up. Young turtles eat mostly insects and earthworms, and adults tend to eat more plants, berries and mushrooms. In captivity, adults also eat invertebrates.

COOL FACTS:

- In 2007, the three-toed box turtle became Missouri's state reptile.
- You can determine the approximate age of a three-toed box turtle by counting the rings of an individual scute.
- By looking at the plastron of an adult box turtle, you can identify its gender. A female's plastron is flat while that of a male's is concave (bowed in).

4½ to 5 inches long

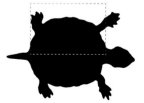

The bottom shell (plastron) of a box turtle has a hinge, allowing it to open and close like a box. In Missouri, only box, mud and musk turtles have hinged plastrons.

Ornate Box Turtle

SPECIES:
Terrapene ornata ornata

This small land turtle has a dark, domed, ornately decorated top shell (carapace) with yellow streaks radiating from its center and a wide broken stripe running down the carapace length. The head, neck and legs can have yellow spots. The bottom shell (plastron) is hinged and has distinct radiating dark lines.

HABITAT AND FOOD:

Ornate box turtles are more commonly found in Missouri's prairie regions and occasionally in the Ozarks. They live in open habitats such as prairies, brushy areas, open fields and south-facing glades. They feed mainly on insects such as grasshoppers, beetles and caterpillars, but also eat fruits such as mulberries and wild strawberries.

COOL FACTS:

• Females begin to breed at eight to 11 years of age.
• Ornate box turtles can live for 30 to 50 years.

4 to 5½ inches long

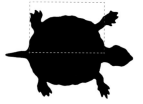

The best way to tell an ornate box turtle from a three-toed box turtle is to look at the bottom shell (plastron). An ornate box turtle has distinct dark markings on the plastron compared with the plain or faintly lined plastron of the three-toed box turtle.

Also, an ornate box turtle has no raised ridge on the top shell (carapace), but a three-toed box turtle does.

Red-eared Slider

SPECIES:
Trachemys scripta elegans

A large red patch behind each eye gives the "red-eared" slider its name. This medium-sized aquatic turtle has an olive-brown to dark green top shell (carapace) with yellow stripes. The bottom shell (plastron) is mostly yellow with a dark spot on each scale. The head, neck and legs are dark green with yellow stripes.

HABITAT AND FOOD:

Red-eared sliders are found across the state except for a few northern counties. They live in streams, sloughs and lakes. They prefer water bodies with mud bottoms, lots of aquatic vegetation and plenty of basking logs or rocks. Red-eared sliders feed on both small animals and plants.

COOL FACTS:

- The name "slider" comes from this turtle's talent for quickly sliding off basking sites when approached.
- An old slider, particularly a male, tends to develop more black pigment on its head and loses its red "ears."
- A turtle's real "ears" are tiny round eardrums (tympanums) on the sides of its head.

5 to 11 inches long

These colorful turtles have been the targets of illegal collection. It is against the law to sell or trade Missouri turtles without proper permits.

89

Spiny Softshell

SPECIES:
Apalone spinifera

Unlike turtles with hard bony shells, this medium-to-large aquatic turtle has a flat, flexible, leathery brown top shell (carapace). In contrast, the bottom shell (plastron) is quite small and is a light cream color. This turtle has a light stripe running from the eye down the neck. It has small spines or bumps on the front edge of the carapace.

HABITAT AND FOOD:

Softshells are found in large streams and rivers (especially the Missouri and Mississippi) throughout the state. They prefer rivers with sandy or muddy bottoms. They bask less frequently than other turtles and will dart into the water when approached. Softshells are true carnivores, eating fish, crayfish, salamanders, frogs, tadpoles, snails and aquatic insects.

COOL FACTS:

- A spiny softshell can bite at a moment's notice. With its long neck, this turtle is difficult to handle without being bitten.
- All softshell turtles, including spiny softshells, are game species and can be harvested for food with proper permits.

7 to 17 inches long

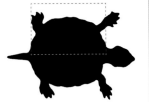

The spiny softshell turtle uses its long neck and pointed nose as a snorkel to breathe while the rest of its body remains buried under mud or sand in shallow waters.

Eastern Collared Lizard

SPECIES:
Crotaphytus collaris

Two distinct black rings around the neck, forming a double "collar," give this large colorful long-tailed lizard its name. Adult males are tan to green and especially bright during the breeding season. Females are light brown to yellow-tan. Young lizards have alternating dark and yellow bands across the back.

HABITAT AND FOOD:

These uncommon lizards live only on limestone, sandstone and granite glades (dry, rocky openings in woodlands on south- and southwest-facing slopes) in parts of southern Missouri. Eastern collared lizards do not do well in captivity. They are best left in their natural glade habitats. They feed on a variety of insects such as beetles, moths, spiders and grasshoppers. Larger lizards eat small snakes and other lizards.

COOL FACTS:

- This is Missouri's largest lizard.
- Collared lizards need to spend a lot of time in the sunlight. Their populations have been known to decline if their glade habitats becomes too shaded with trees. Good glade management helps these animals thrive.

8 to 11¾ inches long

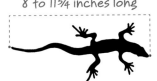

When escaping a predator, a collared lizard can hold its body upright, running very fast on only its hind legs.

92

Prairie Lizard (formerly called Northern Fence Lizard)

SPECIES:
Sceloporus consobrinus

This small, light-to-dark brown lizard has rough scales and two rows of dark arches or "Vs" along the back that meet at the tail. These markings are more obvious on females. Males have dark, metallic blue patches on the throat and belly during the breeding season. Females may have orange or red at the base of the tail.

HABITAT AND FOOD:

Prairie lizards are found across Missouri except for the northwestern quarter of the state. They live in open forests or along edges of woodlands and fields. You may see them climbing fallen trees, rocks, brush piles, landscaping timbers and split rail fences. Prairie lizards feed on a variety of insects and spiders.

COOL FACTS:

- Prairie lizards (along with eastern collared lizards and Texas horned lizards) are closely related to tropical iguanas.
- These are short-lived reptiles. Herpetologists have learned that most prairie lizards do not live longer than three years.

4 to 7¼ inches long

During the breeding season, in the presence of a female, a male often bobs its head and even does pushups, most likely to show off its blue patches.

Little Brown Skink (formerly called Ground Skink)

SPECIES:
Scincella lateralis

The legs of this lizard are smaller than most, giving it a short, snake-like appearance. This small, sleek, dark gray or brown lizard has shiny scales. A wide dark stripe extends along each side of the back from the nose to the middle of the tail. The belly is light gray.

HABITAT AND FOOD:

Little brown skinks are common across Missouri except for some northern parts of the state. They live in wooded areas and can be found crawling in leaf litter and on rocks and logs. They eat a variety of small insects, spiders and earthworms.

COOL FACTS:

- The little brown skink is Missouri's smallest lizard.
- This is one of six skink species in the state. The word "skink" is a shortened version of the family name Scincidae, which is pronounced "Skink-a-day."

3 to 5⅛ inches long

The female little brown skink keeps eggs inside its body longer than most lizards. This allows the eggs to hatch in only 22 days.

Five-lined Skink

SPECIES:
Plestiodon fasciatus

Females and young of this species have five distinct light lines running down a dark back, giving this lizard its name. These small brown skinks have smooth, shiny scales. Males have faint or no lines down the back, but can have bright red-orange on the head. Young lizards have bright blue tails.

HABITAT AND FOOD:

Five-lined skinks are common throughout most of Missouri except for some counties bordering Iowa. They live in open wooded areas, on rocky south-facing hillsides and along wooded bluffs. They are commonly found crawling on bases of trees, leaves, rocks, logs and stumps. Around houses, they are often seen crawling along rock gardens, decks and foundations. Five-lined skinks feed on a variety of insects and spiders.

COOL FACT:

- Females can detect rotten eggs within 24 hours of going bad. To prevent a bad egg from harming the other eggs in a nest, the female will eat it.

5 to 8 1/16 inches long

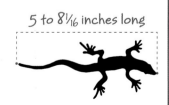

Like all skinks, the five-lined skink can break off its tail to escape capture. The tail will grow back.

Broad-headed Skink

SPECIES:
Plestiodon laticeps

These small to medium-sized lizards have smooth, shiny, brown scales. The male is olive-brown with few or no stripes. The head is vivid orange-red and the jaws appear swollen during the breeding season. The female has light stripes along the back and a wide dark stripe along each side. The young, like those of five-lined skinks, are black with five light stripes and bright blue tails.

HABITAT AND FOOD:

Broad-headed skinks live in cavities, stumps, large logs or lumber piles in forests and woodlands in the southern two-thirds of the state. They eat a variety of insects and spiders.

COOL FACTS:

- Some people call these skinks "scorpions" or think they are venomous. Actually, they are harmless reptiles!
- Female broad-headed skinks may sometimes share nest sites with other females.

6½ to 12¾ inches long

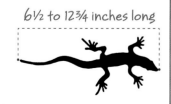

Broad-headed skinks and five-lined skinks can look very much alike. You can tell them apart by counting the scales along the upper lip (labial scales). The broad-headed skink has eight and the five-lined skink has seven.

101

Six-lined Racerunner

SPECIES:
Aspidoscelis sexlineata

This brown-to-black, long, slender, fast-moving lizard usually has six light yellow lines running down the back and tail. Some individuals have yellow to greenish yellow along the sides. On the back and sides, scales are small and rough. Belly scales are large and rectangular. The male has a broad head, which is green to blue-gray.

HABITAT AND FOOD:

Six-lined racerunners are found across most of the state except for north-central Missouri. They live in open areas with loose soil or sand and little vegetation. You can observe them on rocky south-facing hillsides, open floodplains, glades and prairies. They eat invertebrates such as insects, spiders and scorpions.

COOL FACTS:

- The six-lined racerunner is Missouri's only member of a lizard group known as "whiptails" or "racerunners."
- These lizards shelter in burrows and under rocks, and don't hesitate to enter creeks or pools of water to escape.

6 to 9⅞ inches long

This lizard—with its long tail and strong hind limbs—is extremely fast and difficult to catch!

Western Slender Glass Lizard

SPECIES:
Ophisaurus attenuatus attenuatus

This is indeed a lizard and not a snake! The western slender glass lizard has smooth scales and a light brown body. It has a brown stripe down the center of the back and several thin dark stripes along the sides. It has a pointed head and a long tail, which is often two-thirds the length of its body.

HABITAT AND FOOD:

Western slender glass lizards live throughout the state but are uncommon. You might see one on a prairie, a pasture, in open woods or on a dry rocky hillside. Glass lizards can burrow in loose soil and also make use of small mammal burrows. They eat grasshoppers, crickets, spiders, eggs of other lizards and occasionally eggs of ground-nesting birds.

COOL FACT:

- Glass lizard tails break off quite easily, sometimes in several pieces. When caught, the glass lizard may thrash violently enough to break its tail off to help it escape.

22 to 28 inches long

This legless lizard is different from snakes in three ways. It has moveable eyelids, a detachable and regenerating tail, and ear openings. Snakes lack these three features.

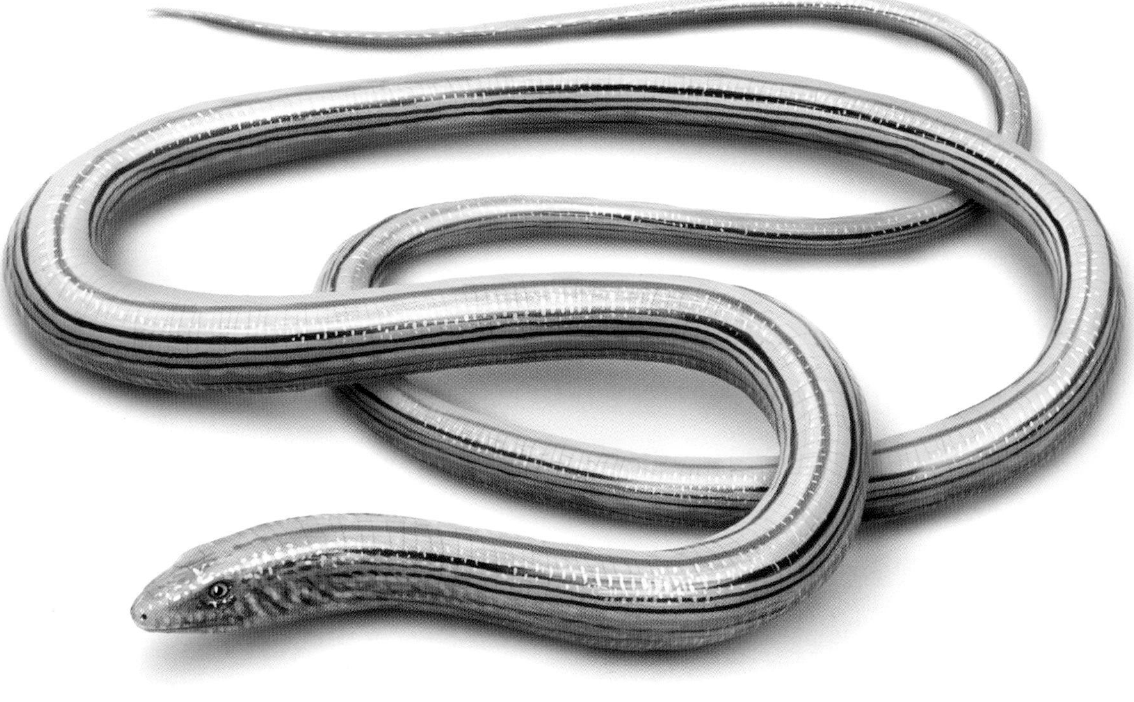

Western Wormsnake

SPECIES:
Carphophis vermis

The top half of this small snake is a completely different color from the bottom. The top is solid black or dark purplish brown. The belly half is solid pink. The western wormsnake has small eyes and a flat, pointed head. It has smooth scales and a tail that ends with a sharp point.

HABITAT AND FOOD:

Western wormsnakes are found across the state. They live on wooded or open rocky hillsides. They also can be found along the edge of forests and in moist ravines. They are rarely seen above ground and are commonly found beneath rocks, logs and damp leaf litter. They eat mostly earthworms and soft-bodied insects.

COOL FACTS:

- This snake's sharp tail is harmless—there is no such thing as a "stinging" snake.
- The western wormsnake spends most of the time below ground or hiding under rocks or logs.

7½ to 14⅞ inches long

This secretive snake gets its name because of its worm-like body, pink belly and small size—and it also eats worms!

Ring-necked Snake

SPECIES:
Diadophis punctatus

This small snake gets its name from the distinctive light yellow or light orange ring around its neck. Its back has smooth, dark gray scales. Its belly is bright yellow starting at the head, then becomes orange to bright red at the tail. The belly also is covered with black dots.

HABITAT AND FOOD:

The ring-necked snake is found across the state. It lives in prairies, pastures, open woods, dry rocky glades and along woodland edges. These snakes are most often found below rocks, logs and bark and in piles of lumber. They feed mostly on earthworms, but also will eat insects and small salamanders.

COOL FACTS:

- The ring-necked snake may be the most common snake in Missouri.
- These snakes rarely bite, but can release a strong unpleasant smell from glands near the tail.
- They may live 10 to 12 years.

10 to 19 inches long

When captured, this snake curls up its bright red tail in an effort to startle a predator. This also can misdirect an attack away from the head to the less vital tail.

Eastern Yellow-bellied Racer

SPECIES:
Coluber constrictor flaviventris

Adult and young eastern yellow-bellied racers look completely different. The adults are usually solid olive-gray with cream-yellow bellies. They also are faintly green-blue where the sides and belly meet. Juveniles, however, are light gray with small, irregular, dark brown blotches and spots. This medium-to-large, smooth-scaled snake has large eyes compared with other snakes.

HABITAT AND FOOD:

Eastern yellow-bellied racers are found across the state. They live in prairies, pastures, brushy areas and along the edges of forests. They eat a wide variety of prey, including small rodents, lizards, small snakes, frogs, birds and insects.

COOL FACTS:

- Some people call this snake the "blue racer."
- Contrary to popular belief, this snake does not chase people. It will vibrate its tail when alarmed and can dart away quickly in any direction to escape.
- The eastern yellow-bellied racer bites easily and rarely calms down in captivity.

30 to 52 inches long

Although constrictor is part of its scientific name, this snake does not constrict its prey—it eats its food alive.

Black Ratsnake

SPECIES:
Pantherophis obsoletus

The adult black ratsnake is nearly solid black on top, but with a white chin and lower jaw. The hatchling, however, is light gray on top with large black blotches. The hatchling also has a black stripe that wraps around the face through the eyes, like a narrow superhero mask. The skin between the scales along the sides is mainly white, but may have some red coloration as well.

HABITAT AND FOOD:

Black ratsnakes are common across the state. They live on rocky wooded hillsides and in wooded areas along rivers and streams. They can be found on the ground and in trees, brush piles and old farm buildings. Adults eat mostly rodents, birds and bird eggs. Young black ratsnakes eat frogs, lizards and insects.

COOL FACTS:

• The black ratsnake is one of Missouri's largest snakes.
• Black ratsnakes kill their prey by constriction.
• In the heat of the summer, these snakes become nocturnal hunters.

42 to 84 inches long

The black ratsnake is one of the few snakes that can climb extensively in trees. You can sometimes see one basking on tree branches.

Eastern Hog-nosed Snake

SPECIES:
Heterodon platirhinos

This medium-sized snake gets its name from its pig-like, upturned snout. Individuals can be solid dark brown-to-gray or reddish with large spots or blotches along the back. This snake has two elongated black patches, one behind each jaw.

HABITAT AND FOOD:

Eastern hog-nosed snakes are common across the state. They live in rocky wooded hillsides, old fields, open woods and sandy floodplains. They eat mostly amphibians, including toads, frogs and sometimes salamanders.

COOL FACTS:

- This is one of three hog-nosed snakes in the state. The other two are the dusty hog-nosed and the plains hog-nosed.
- Because of the way it can inflate its body or flatten its head to scare off predators, some people call the eastern hog-nosed snake a "puff adder" or "spreadhead."
- Hog-nosed snakes are one of the few predators of toads.

22 to 33 inches long

This snake carries out an elaborate act to evade predators or intruders, including people. Turn to page 19 to see what a good actor it can be!

Prairie Kingsnake

SPECIES:
Lampropeltis calligaster calligaster

This medium-sized, tan or gray snake has a brown "V" on its head with the bottom pointing toward its back. It has brown or reddish brown saddle-shaped blotches along its top and sides, and has smooth scales. The blotches on top are larger than those on the sides. The yellow belly has rectangular brown markings.

HABITAT AND FOOD:

Prairie kingsnakes are common across the state. They live in native prairies, along open fields and pastures, rocky wooded hillsides and near farm buildings. They feed on mice, lizards and small snakes.

COOL FACTS:

- Some people confuse the prairie kingsnake for the Great Plains ratsnake, but it does not have the "V" on the head.
- The prairie kingsnake kills food by constriction.
- When captured, this snake will vibrate its tail and may bite, but it is nonvenomous.

30 to 51 inches long

Some people mistake the prairie kingsnake for a copperhead. The kingsnake's markings are saddle-shaped, whereas the markings on the copperhead look more like hourglass crossbands. Because kingsnakes eat lots of mice, they provide an important rodent-control service.

Speckled Kingsnake

SPECIES:
Lampropeltis getula holbrooki

Each smooth black scale on this medium-sized snake has a single white or yellow dot, making the snake look speckled. The belly is predominantly yellow with large black rectangular markings. Young speckled kingsnakes may have clusters of dots along the back that resemble yellow bars. As the snake ages, these markings change to a more evenly speckled pattern.

HABITAT AND FOOD:

The speckled kingsnake is common across the state. It lives in prairies, rocky wooded hillsides and along the edges of forests, swamps and marshes. These snakes are highly secretive, but can be found under rocks, logs, rotting stumps and in small animal burrows. They eat rodents, small birds and their eggs, lizards and other snakes.

COOL FACTS:

- Another common name for this snake is the "salt and pepper snake."
- The speckled kingsnake will shake its tail when captured, but usually calms down quickly.
- Kingsnakes eat other snakes, including venomous ones. They kill prey by constriction.

36 to 60 inches long

The speckled kingsnake is immune to the venom of native Missouri pit vipers.

Red Milksnake

SPECIES:
Lampropeltis triangulum syspila

This beautiful medium-sized snake has a white or light tan background with 20 to 30 red to orange-red blotches along the back, each of which is bordered in black. It is medium-sized, has smooth scales and red eyes, and its belly is white with dark, irregular markings.

HABITAT AND FOOD:

Although red milksnakes are common throughout Missouri on rocky south-facing hillsides and glades, they are very secretive. You might find one by looking under a rock or log—just be sure to put the rock or log back as you found it. Red milksnakes eat lizards, mice and small snakes.

COOL FACTS:

- The name "milksnake" comes from a mistaken belief that these snakes drink milk from cows.
- The red milksnake is one of three kingsnake species in Missouri. They all eat other snakes, including venomous ones.

Some people confuse the milksnake for the venomous coral snake, which is not even found in Missouri. Because of this confusion, milksnakes are often needlessly killed. This rhyme can help you tell the two snakes apart:
"Red meets black is a friend of Jack" = Red Milksnake
"Red meets yellow can kill a fellow" = Coral Snake

28 to 33 inches long

Northern Watersnake

SPECIES:
Nerodia sipedon sipedon

This medium-to-large stout snake can be gray or brown with several dark brown saddle-shaped bands across the body. These bands break up into blotches on the lower portion of the body. This snake has keeled scales. The belly is cream colored with reddish brown half moons along each side.

HABITAT AND FOOD:

Northern watersnakes are common across the state. Their habitats include creeks, rivers, sloughs, ponds, lakes and swamps. You can sometimes see them sunning themselves on logs, rocks or in trees overhanging water. They primarily eat small fish, but also will eat amphibians.

COOL FACTS:

- Like many other snakes, northern watersnakes release a foul-smelling odor for defense.
- Females give birth to a litter of six to 66 live young.

24 to 54 inches long

The northern watersnake is one of five harmless Missouri watersnakes. Unlike the cottonmouth, which is a venomous, semi-aquatic snake that cannot climb well, female watersnakes climb trees to release pheromones to attract males or to bask in the sun.

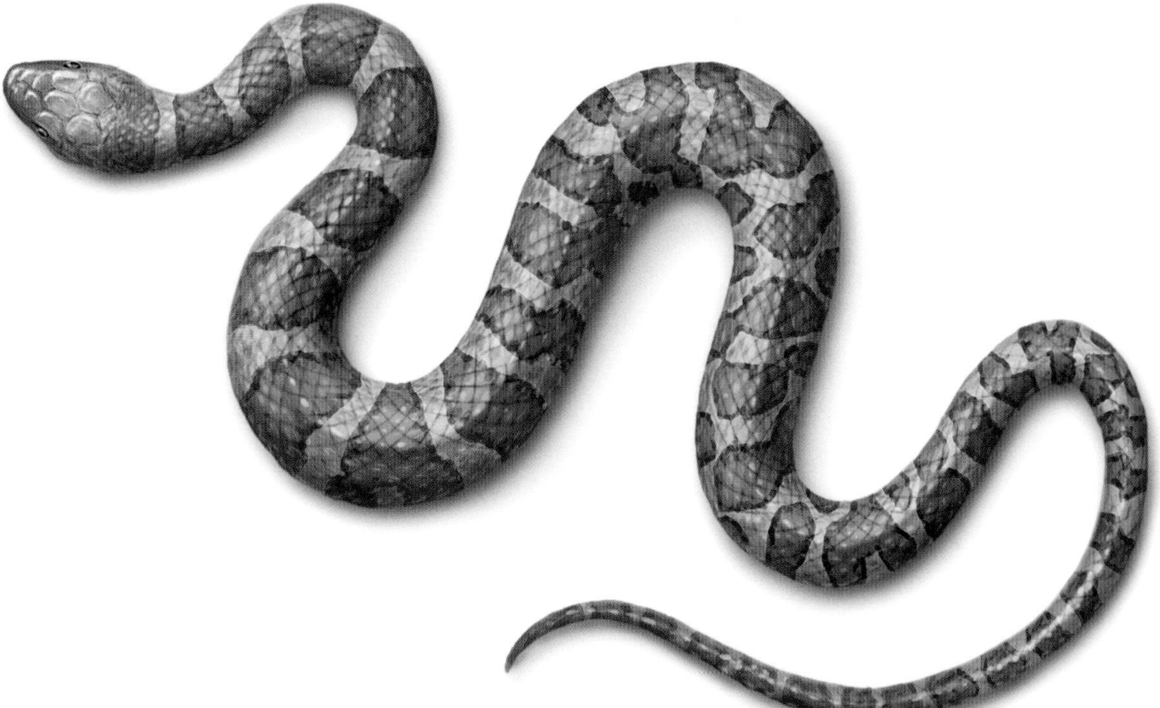

Rough Greensnake

SPECIES:
Opheodrys aestivus

People sometimes overlook this snake because its vivid green color helps it blend in with vines, leaves and other plant parts. Its belly is a light cream color, and its scales are weakly keeled. The tail is extremely long and easily can be one-third of the entire length of the snake.

HABITAT AND FOOD:

Rough greensnakes are found across most of Missouri except for the northernmost counties. They live in dense vegetation along creeks, rivers, forested hillsides and river bluffs. They feed on insects and spiders.

COOL FACTS:

- Greensnakes are the only green-colored snakes in Missouri. They are nonvenomous and harmless.
- The tails of these snakes are longer than those of other snakes. Their long tails allow them to be excellent climbers.

22 to 30 inches long

This small, thin, tree-climbing snake evades predators by blending in with green vegetation and swaying its head to resemble a leaf waving in the breeze.

Orange-striped Ribbonsnake

(formerly called Western Ribbon Snake)

SPECIES:
Thamnophis proximus proximus

Three prominent stripes run down the length of this medium-sized, thin snake. The stripe on the top of the back is orange to orange-yellow. The two stripes along the sides are yellow to white. There is a small yellow or orange spot on top of the black head. The background color is dark brown to black, occasionally with white flecks. This snake has keeled scales.

HABITAT AND FOOD:

Rarely far from water, orange-striped ribbonsnakes are found across the state on or near prairies, marshes, streams, lakes and ponds. They easily take to water; it is not uncommon to see them swimming along the water's edge. Earthworms, minnows and amphibians are their common prey.

COOL FACTS:

- Orange-striped ribbonsnakes look a lot like gartersnakes, but the ribbon-like ribbonsnakes are thinner.
- These snakes can be very quick and hard to capture.
- The female gives birth to a litter of four to 28 live snakes.

21 to 31 inches long

To avoid the worst of summertime heat, these and many other snakes become nocturnal during the hottest months of the year.

127

Eastern Gartersnake

SPECIES: *Thamnophis sirtalis sirtalis*	These medium-sized, stout snakes are mostly solid black, brown or olive-green. Some individuals have a red-checkered pattern on the sides. There are three distinct stripes running the length of the body that can be yellow, brown, green or blue.
HABITAT AND FOOD:	Eastern gartersnakes live throughout Missouri in a wide variety of habitats, including damp woods and near marshes, swamps, ponds, creeks and rivers. They feed on amphibians, earthworms and minnows.
COOL FACTS:	• The name "gartersnake" comes from the resemblance to the garters or bands men used to hold their socks up in the late 1800s and early 1900s.
	• Like other snakes, gartersnakes can release a foul-smelling odor when captured.
	• Gartersnakes look a lot like ribbonsnakes, but garters have heavier bodies and lack a distinct yellow or orange spot on the head.

18 to 41 5/8 inches long

This is most likely North America's most common snake—you often can find one in any moist or wet habitat, including in yards near creeks or ponds.

Copperhead

SPECIES:
Agkistrodon contortrix

This beautiful medium-to-large snake has a light copper-colored head and light and dark copper-brown markings. Like other venomous snakes, it has a flattened, triangular head and vertical pupils. It has two small dark spots near the middle of its head. On young copperheads, the tail tip is yellow, but the color fades to black as the snakes get older.

HABITAT AND FOOD:

Copperheads are found across most of Missouri except for the extreme northern counties. They live on rocky wooded hillsides, along brushy creeks and near abandoned buildings. Adults eat primarily rodents, while young copperheads feed mostly on amphibians and lizards.

COOL FACTS:

• The copperhead is one of five VENOMOUS snakes in Missouri. Always leave them alone!

• Copperheads are not aggressive and usually remain motionless when approached.

• Copperheads can live 20 or more years in the wild.

24 to 43 inches long

Copperheads have a distinctive "chocolate kisses" pattern along their sides. The tips of the kisses meet to form hourglass crossbands. This pattern helps copperheads blend in with forest leaf litter.

131

Western Cottonmouth

SPECIES:
Agkistrodon piscivorus leucostoma

Like other venomous snakes, this large, heavy-bodied snake has a flattened, triangular head. The adult is mostly solid black or has a dark mottled pattern with a white upper lip. A young cottonmouth has a distinct pattern and a bright yellow tail. The belly is heavily mottled.

HABITAT AND FOOD:

Cottonmouths are found only in the southern third of the state, primarily in the southeastern corner. They live in swamps and remote, clear Ozark streams. They seek out isolated areas and avoid places frequented by people. Cottonmouths eat fish, frogs, rodents and small birds.

COOL FACTS:

- This is Missouri's only semi-aquatic VENOMOUS snake.
- Contrary to an old mistaken belief, cottonmouths do not have nests in the water
- Cottonmouths can bite under water.
- These snakes often swim with most of the body at or above the water surface, while most nonvenomous watersnakes swim with only the head above water.

32 to 42 5/8 inches long

The name "cottonmouth" comes from the white lining of the mouth. The open mouth is a defensive display, warning you not to come closer.

133

Timber Rattlesnake

SPECIES:
Crotalus horridus

This large, stout snake has a dark gray or dull yellow background color and has a large tan segmented rattle at the end of its black tail. In addition to a rust-colored stripe down the center of the back, the timber rattlesnake has jagged markings that can loosely resemble black lightning bolts across its back and down its sides.

HABITAT AND FOOD:

Very secretive and shy, these uncommon snakes live along rocky wooded hillsides and rocky bluffs. While they have been found in nearly every county in the state, they are not found in large numbers. They prey on mice, small rabbits and occasionally birds.

COOL FACTS:

- This is Missouri's largest VENOMOUS snake and one of the state's three rattlesnakes. The other two are the western pygmy rattlesnake and the eastern massasauga rattlesnake.
- Females are not able to breed until they are five to nine years old.
- Timber rattlesnakes may live as long as 30 years.

36 to 47 inches long

A rattlesnake's rattle is made of hollow interlocking segments of keratin, which is the same material as your fingernails!

GLOSSARY

Amphibian

"Dual life." Vertebrate that is ectothermic and spends part of its life in the water and part of its life on land. Toads, frogs and salamanders are amphibians. Compare to reptile.

Aquatic

Describes plants or animals that live in water.

Arthropods

Invertebrates such as insects, arachnids and crustaceans that have a segmented body and jointed legs. A wide variety of arthropods are food for herps.

Basking

Activity used primarily by reptiles to expose their bodies to the sun to raise or maintain their body temperature.

Brumation

Overwintering or hibernation-like state that herps and other ectothermic animals enter to survive cold weather.

Camouflage

Body shape, coloration or patterns that allow an animal to blend into its surroundings.

Carapace

Top half of a turtle's shell that is actually the backbone and flattened ribs.

Claws
Hard sharp tips on the end of reptiles' toes.

Cloaca
The common chamber through which the urinary, digestive and reproductive canals discharge their contents.

Constriction
The method some snakes use to kill prey: they coil their bodies around prey and squeeze.

Costal Grooves
The vertical indented lines on the sides of salamanders between the front and back legs.

Diurnal
Describes animals that are active mostly during the day. The opposite of nocturnal.

Ectothermic
A term used for animals that rely on elements of the external environment (for example, sun, water or rocks) to regulate their body temperature. Herps are considered ectothermic. Sometimes confused with the inaccurate term "cold-blooded." Compare to endothermic.

Endangered
A plant or animal with so few individuals that without conservation efforts it could go extinct.

Endothermic

Describes the ability of an animal to regulate its body temperature internally (as by sweating or shivering). Birds and mammals are considered endothermic. Sometimes confused with the inaccurate term "warm-blooded." Compare to ectothermic.

Genus

A group of plants or animals with one or more common characteristics between the ranking of "family" and "species." The genus name is the first part of a creature's scientific name. For example, the ringed salamander (*Ambystoma annulatum*) is in the mole salamander family (Family Ambystomatidae) and belongs to the genus *Ambystoma*.

Glade

A dry rocky opening in woodlands on south- and southwest-facing slopes in parts of eastern and southern Missouri. Glades provide important habitat for many herps, including collared lizards and milksnakes.

Habitat

A specific kind of area (such as a wetland, forest or glade) that provides a plant or animal with food, water, space and shelter. Different herps need different habitats.

Herpetology

The study of amphibians and reptiles.

Herps

Short for amphibians and reptiles.

Imperiled

A plant or animal in peril or in danger of disappearing from an area because of rarity or some factors that threaten its survival.

Invertebrate

Animal without a backbone, including insects, worms, spiders and snails. Invertebrates are important food for herps.

Juvenile

A young animal that is no longer in the larval stage, but has not fully taken on all traits of an adult.

Keeled scale

Scale with a small ridge down the center, resembling the bottom of a keeled boat. Keeled scales are found along the sides and backs of some snakes and lizards.

Keratin

Fibrous protein material that makes up scales, rattlesnake rattles, hair, feathers and our fingernails.

Larva

The early life stage of many animals that undergo metamorphosis. The larval stage of a toad, for example, is a tadpole.

Metamorphosis

The complete change of an organism from larva to adult that may involve several distinct stages.

Neotenic

Sexually mature and able to reproduce, but retaining many larval characteristics. The mudpuppy is an example of a neotenic salamander.

Nocturnal

Describes animals that are active mostly at night, such as a bat or owl. Opposite of diurnal.

Omnivore

Describes an animal that eats plants and other animals.

Overwinter

To enter a hibernation-like state. Herps and other ectothermic animals overwinter to survive very cold weather. Overwintering is also called brumation. Overwintering can involve rapidly lowering the body temperature and slowing metabolism in the winter and rapidly raising the body temperature and metabolism in the spring. Unlike hibernation, moving in or out of overwintering can happen more quickly.

Oviparous

Animals that lay eggs. Young develop in the egg outside the mother's body. Examples include turtles, kingsnakes and lizards. Compare to ovoviviparous.

Ovoviviparous

Animals that retain the eggs in the mother's body during their development. The young emerge from the mother surrounded only by a clear membrane and are fully developed. Examples include venomous snakes, gartersnakes and watersnakes. Compare to oviparous.

Parotoid gland

An external skin gland on toads that looks like a large bump behind each eye. The gland produces a mild poison to deter predators. These glands can make an amphibian look "warty," which may be the reason for the false belief that touching a toad causes warts.

Pheromones

Specialized odors that are released by an animal to attract or stimulate a mate.

Plastron

Bottom half of a turtle's shell.

Poisonous

Term used for plants, mushrooms and animals that are not edible and dangerous to eat or touch. Poison may be produced by glands on the skin of an animal to protect it from being eaten. The only way that something poisonous can hurt you is if you eat or touch it. Compare to venomous.

Reptile

Vertebrate that has scales, is ectothermic and does not have to live in water during its development. Most reptiles (but not all) lay eggs. Compare to amphibian.

Scales

The flat, hardened disks or plates on the outside of the skin of most reptiles. These scales help prevent water loss, give protection and provide coloration.

Scutes

The scales on a turtle's shell.

Species

A category of biological classification immediately below a genus or subgenus. Animals of the same species can interbreed. The genus and species names together make up a creature's scientific name. For example, the ringed salamander belongs to the genus *Ambystoma*, and its full species name is *Ambystoma annulatum*.

Tadpole
Larval stage of a toad or frog. This stage lives under water and breathes through gills. Some people use the word "polliwog" for tadpole.

Terrestrial
"On land." This term is often used to describe animals that live on land rather than in water.

Tympanum
Flat disc behind the eye on toads and frogs that is an external ear drum.

Venomous
Term used for animals that can inflict a toxin by biting or stinging. The venom glands of reptiles are modified salivary glands. Compare to poisonous.

Vent
External opening to the cloaca; also called the anus.

Vertebrate
Animal with a backbone. Herps and humans are examples of vertebrates.

INDEX

SPECIES LIST BY GROUP

SPECIES BY COMMON NAME
(scientific name in parentheses)

For Further Reading and Exploration

FREE PUBLICATIONS FROM THE MISSOURI DEPARTMENT OF CONSERVATION
Order the following free brochures by e-mailing pubstaff@mdc.mo.gov or calling (573) 522-4115 ext. 3630.

Missouri Copperheads, The Lizards of Missouri, Missouri's Toads and Frogs, Missouri's Turtles, Snakes of Missouri

BOOKS AND CDS
FROM THE MISSOURI DEPARTMENT OF CONSERVATION'S NATURE SHOP
Order the following sale items by visiting www.mdcnatureshop.com or calling 877-521-8632.

The Amphibians and Reptiles of Missouri by Tom R. Johnson, 2000. Toads and Frogs in Missouri CD and Poster

OTHER BOOKS

A Field Guide to the Reptiles and Amphibians: Eastern and Central North America
  by Roger Conant and Joseph T. Collins, 1998

National Audubon Society Field Guide to North American Reptiles and Amphibians
  by J. L. Behler and F. W. King, 1997

Reptiles and Amphibians: Golden Guide Series
  by Herbert S. Zim and Hobart M. Smith, revised by Jonathan P. Latimer and Karen Stray Nolting, 2001

Reptiles of North America: A Guide to Field Identification
  by Hobart M. Smith and Edmund D. Brodie, 1982

ORGANIZATIONS AND WEBSITES

MISSOURI

Kansas City Herpetological Society www.kcherp.com

Missouri Department of Conservation www.MissouriConservation.org

Missouri Herpetological Atlas Project www.atlas.moherp.org

St. Louis Herpetological Society www.stlherpsociety.org

NATIONAL

Center for Reptile and Amphibian Conservation and Management herpcenter.ipfw.edu

Chytrid Fungus and Amphibians www.amphibianark.org/the-crisis/chytrid-fungus

ENature www.enature.com

North American Amphibian Monitoring Program www.pwrc.usgs.gov/naamp

Partners in Amphibian and Reptile Conservation (PARC) parcplace.org

Scientific and Common Names of the Reptiles and Amphibians of North America - Explained
ebeltz.net/herps/etymain.html

Society for the Study of Amphibians and Reptiles (SSAR) www.ssarherps.org

150

An avid naturalist and photographer, John Miller enjoys sharing his interest in amphibians and reptiles with others. As the conservation center manager at the Shepherd of the Hills Fish Hatchery, John provides interpretive programs on Missouri's plants and animals, has written articles for *Missouri Conservationist* magazine and has maintained the Missouri Department of Conservation herp display at the Missouri State Fair since 1996. John, his wife Kathy and their dogs live in southwestern Missouri.

MEET THE ILLUSTRATOR

A conservatory-trained pianist, Steve Buchanan left his post as a college music professor to become a nature artist. Painting with his computer, he has created art for books, magazines, T-shirts, posters, product labels and United States postage stamps. He especially liked painting the green frog (above right), imagining it floating in a pond on a hot summer day.

ACKNOWLEDGMENTS

The production team would like to thank the following individuals for their help with this book. Jeff Briggler, state herpetologist, helped select the 50 animals featured, and also provided valuable technical review of the text. Former state herpetologist Tom Johnson reviewed many of the illustrations to make sure they accurately represented the herps in this book. Kate Kelly, resource science assistant, assisted in reviewing the text. Les Fortenberry, graphic designer with the Missouri Department of Conservation, provided the design template for the book and also designed the book's cover. Gratitude also goes to all conservation groups, professionals, landowners and other individuals who work to protect and conserve Missouri's herps and the habitats on which they depend.